THE RESPIRATORY SYSTEM

JOSEPH MIDTHUN   SAMUEL HITI

BUILDING
BLOCKS

SCIENCE

WORLD
BOOK

www.worldbook.com

World Book, Inc.
180 North LaSalle Street
Suite 900
Chicago, Illinois 60601
USA

For information about other World Book publications,
visit our website at www.worldbook.com
or call 1-800-WORLDBK (967-5325).
For information about sales to schools and libraries,
call 1-800-975-3250 (United States),
or 1-800-837-5365 (Canada).

Building Blocks of Science:
  The Respiratory System
ISBN: 978-0-7166-7866-3 (trade, hc.)
ISBN: 978-0-7166-7874-8 (pbk.)
ISBN: 978-0-7166-2957-3 (e-book, EPUB3)

Acknowledgments:
Created by Samuel Hiti and Joseph Midthun
Art by Samuel Hiti
Text by Joseph Midthun
Special thanks to Syril McNally

TABLE OF CONTENTS

What Is Respiration? 4

The Respiratory System 6

Inhalation and Exhalation.....................8

Into the Nose 10

Down the Lungs 12

...And into the Blood............................14

Exercise and Altitude 16

Lung Defenses 20

Lung Problems 24

Tough Lungs 28

Glossary..30

Find Out More....................................31

Index 32

There is a glossary on page 30. Terms defined in the glossary are in type **that looks like this** on their first appearance.

The **cells** of the body need oxygen to break down food and use energy.

As this happens, wastes like **carbon dioxide** gas are formed.

When you breathe out, you get rid of carbon dioxide.

This process of using oxygen is called **respiration**.

Your lungs and other body parts allow you to breathe.

Together, these body parts make up the **respiratory system!**

THE RESPIRATORY SYSTEM

Several **organs** and muscles make up the respiratory system.

The nose and mouth connect to a large tube called the **trachea,** or windpipe.

The trachea begins at the back of the mouth, runs down the neck into the upper chest, and splits into two smaller tubes...

...called **bronchi.**

Each of these tubes leads to the lungs.

Muscles and bones also play an important role in respiration.

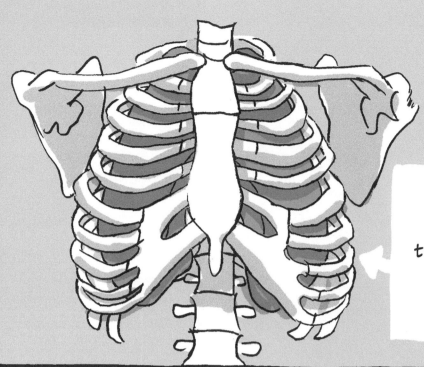

The chest wall includes bones that form a protective cage around the **chest cavity,** muscles associated with these bones, and the abdominal muscles.

The **diaphragm** is a dome-shaped sheet of muscle that separates the chest area from the abdomen.

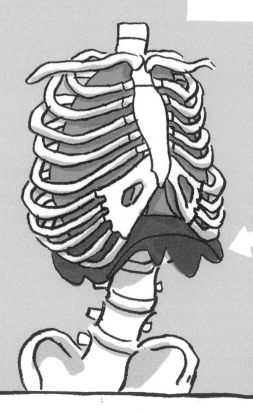

Without these bones and muscles, you would not be able to take a single breath!

INHALATION AND EXHALATION

Breathing consists of two acts: breathing in, or **inhalation**...

...and breathing out, or **exhalation**.

When you inhale, the diaphragm and the muscles of the chest wall contract.

This action lifts the ribs and makes the chest cavity longer and wider, causing the lungs to expand and draw in air.

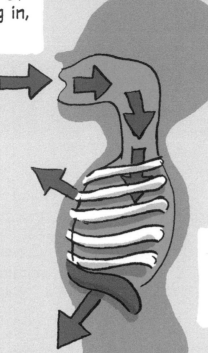

The lower parts of each lung contain elastic fibers in the walls of the airways.

When you inhale and the lungs expand, these elastic **tissues** stretch—

—like an inflating balloon.

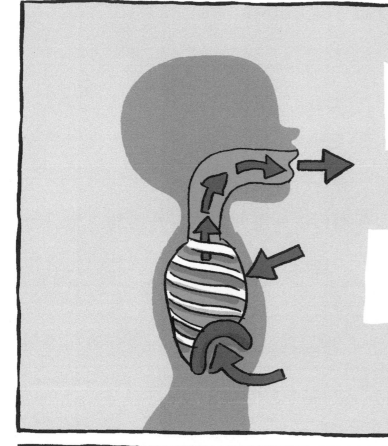

When you exhale, the diaphragm and the rib muscles relax.

The elastic tissues of the lung shrink, pulling the walls of the rib cage with them.

This shrinking of the lungs pushes air out of the body—

—like a deflating balloon!

sqeep

When you finish exhaling, the process starts over again!

But that's not all that happens when you breathe!

INTO THE NOSE...

I don't just hang around on your face, looking pretty –

–I have a very important job.

Your nose acts like a filter, cleaning the air before it passes down your throat into your lungs.

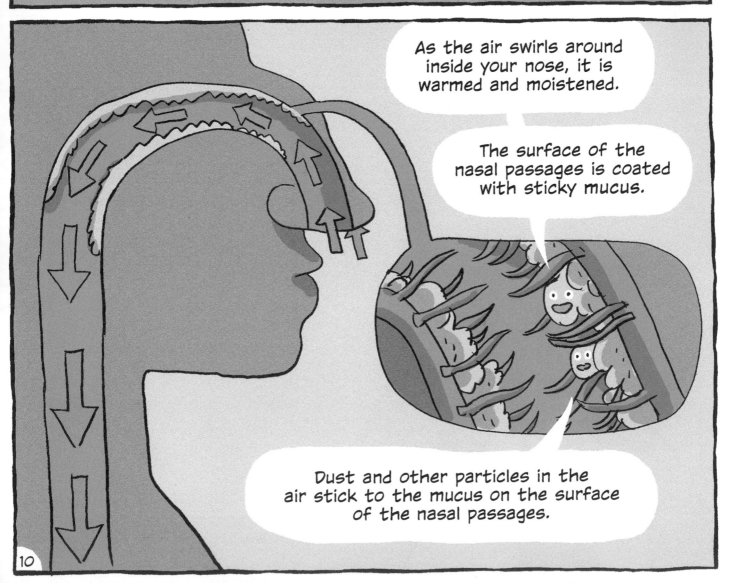

As the air swirls around inside your nose, it is warmed and moistened.

The surface of the nasal passages is coated with sticky mucus.

Dust and other particles in the air stick to the mucus on the surface of the nasal passages.

Some of the particles coming into the nose are **bacteria** and other **microbes**—

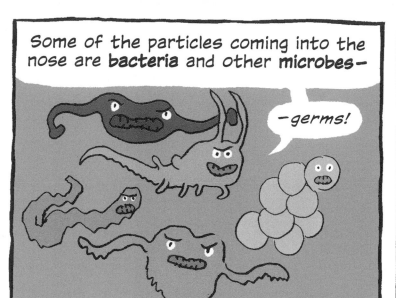

—germs!

Most of these microbes are harmless, but a few can cause infections and disease.

My throat hurts.

Mucus contains special cells that can destroy dangerous microbes.

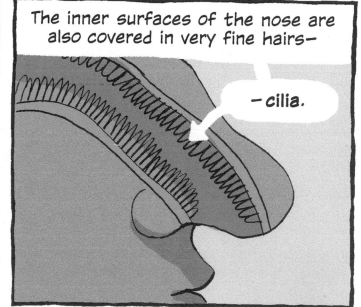

CURSES!

We'll be back!

NO!

The inner surfaces of the nose are also covered in very fine hairs—

—cilia.

As you breathe, the cilia act like a duster.

They wave back and forth, helping to collect dust, bacteria, and mucus, and keep the nasal passages clean.

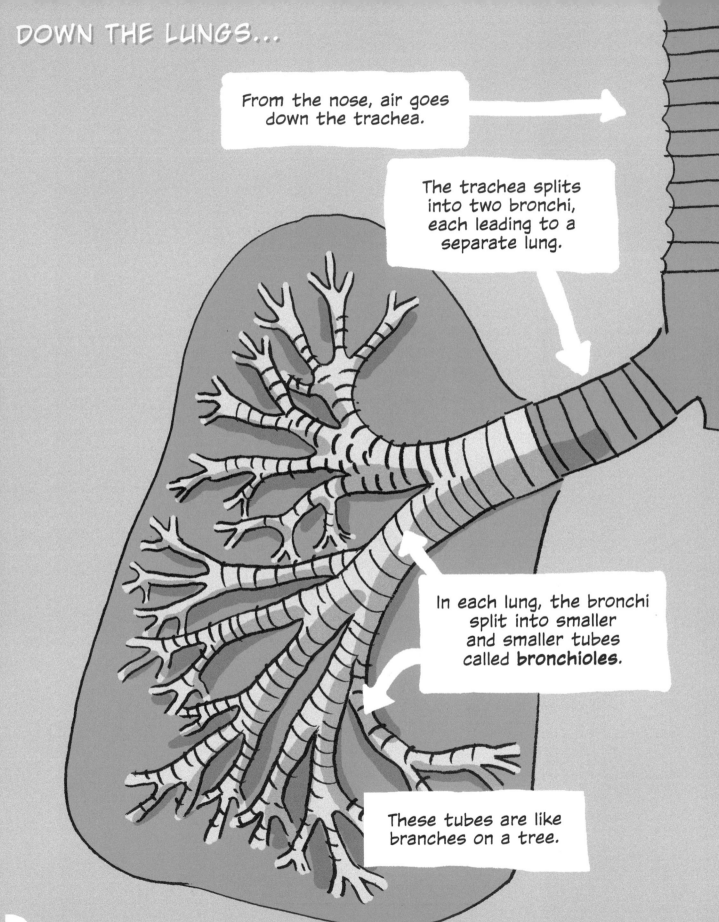

From the nose, air goes down the trachea.

The trachea splits into two bronchi, each leading to a separate lung.

In each lung, the bronchi split into smaller and smaller tubes called **bronchioles**.

These tubes are like branches on a tree.

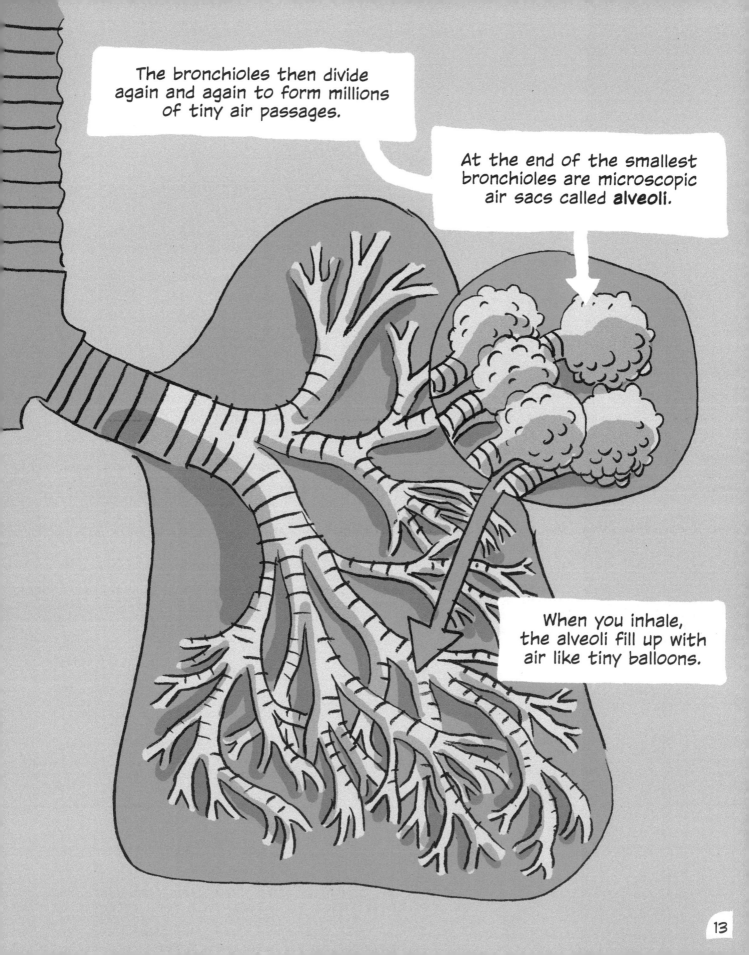

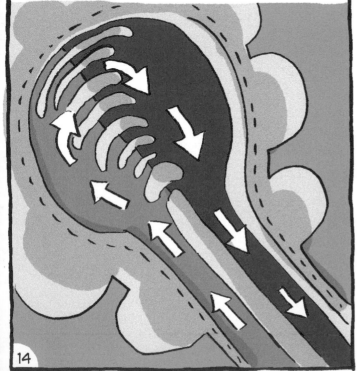

Through the power of the circulatory system, oxygen is transported to your cells by your heart and blood.

At the same time, waste gases like carbon dioxide pass from the cells into the blood...

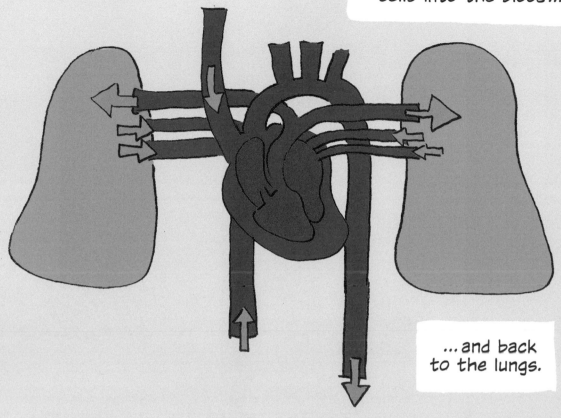

...and back to the lungs.

The waste gases are then transferred through the capillaries into your alveoli...

...and back out of your nose or mouth.

Exhalation!

Sometimes, the body has to work harder to get enough air—

—like when you exercise!

When you are at rest, the amount of oxygen in your muscles is quite high.

I NEED TO TAKE A BREATHER!

But when you're active, your muscles use more oxygen, so you breathe faster and deeper.

PHEW!

Plop

Mount Everest is the tallest peak above sea level on Earth...

At the top, about 9,000 meters, there is only a fourth as much oxygen as there is at sea level!

Very few people can survive the climb to the top of Everest without breathing equipment.

Yet, some people live at heights of about 3,900 meters above sea level, and most humans can get used to living at this height.

19

You are surrounded by germs, and sometimes they get into your nose, mouth, and throat.

And when we get in, we'll make you sick!

Your body tries to kick out these invaders. The lining of your nose becomes inflamed and produces large amounts of mucus to flush out the germs. That's why your nose gets stuffy.

20

The cause of these symptoms is often a tiny **virus**—a germ even smaller than bacteria.

wipe

About 200 different kinds of virus are known to cause colds.

Even when you are healthy, your body works to prevent dust and germs from getting inside.

When something irritates your nose or throat, you cough – or sneeze.

cough cough

When you cough, your stomach and diaphragm muscles contract suddenly...

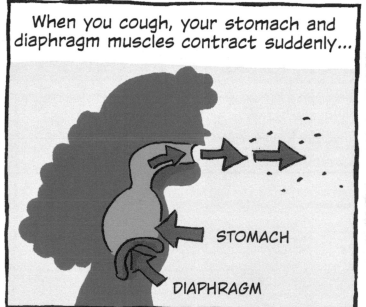

STOMACH

DIAPHRAGM

...sending a high-speed jet of air up your throat and out of your mouth.

A sneeze is similar to a cough, but the air goes out through the nose rather than the mouth.

AH-CHOO!

When germs do get past the nose, your lungs have special defenses to kick them out and keep you from getting sick.

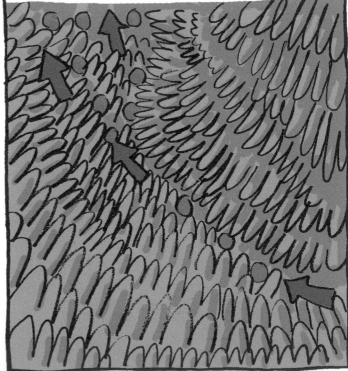

Just like your nose, the lungs contain cilia that move back and forth, gradually pushing any particles trapped in the mucus up and out of the trachea.

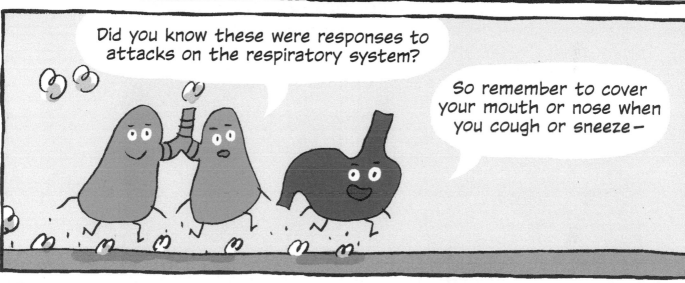

Flu is another disease caused by viruses...

...and it also affects the upper respiratory tract.

The flu virus invades the cells lining these areas and multiplies.

As the body works to fight the virus, you may have symptoms like aching muscles, fatigue, and a high temperature.

Pneumonia is an infection of the lungs often caused by bacteria.

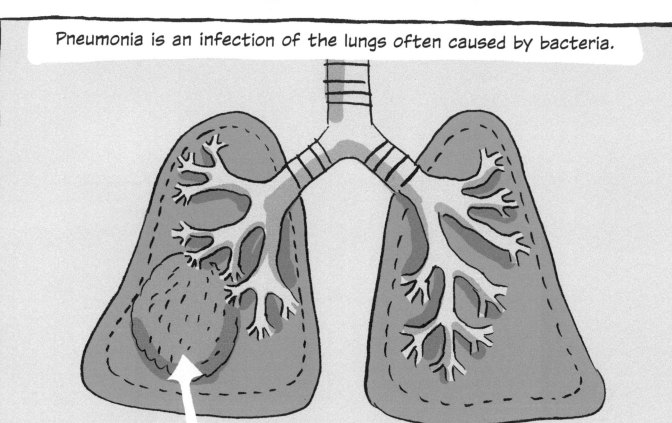

When you have pneumonia, your lung tissues become inflamed.

Luckily, modern **antibiotics** can kill bacteria in the lungs.

The best way to prevent yourself from getting these bacteria is to wash your hands regularly.

Scrub Scrub

SOAP

An **allergy** is a body reaction that occurs in a person who is sensitive to a certain substance, such as plant pollen.

Or pet hair.

The sensitivity can cause sneezing and other symptoms.

Woof it something I woofed?

Meow don't meow.

People with **asthma** suffer from inflammation of the bronchi, which obstructs airflow.

You okay?

GASP.

When someone has an asthma attack, they can use medicines that decrease constriction in the airways.

These medicines relax small muscles in and around the lungs.

GLOSSARY

allergy a bodily reaction to a particular substance.

alveoli tiny air sacs in the lungs.

antibiotics useful medications for treating infections caused by bacteria.

asthma a condition that makes breathing difficult and causes coughing.

bacterium; bacteria a tiny single-celled organism; more than one bacterium.

blood vessel a hollow tube that carries blood and nutrients through the body.

bronchi airways to the lungs.

bronchiole a small tube that branches off the bronchi.

capillary a blood vessel with a very narrow opening.

carbon dioxide the air that is breathed out of the lungs.

cell the basic unit of all living things.

chest cavity the hollow space between the neck and the abdomen. The chest cavity is enclosed by the ribs.

cilia tiny, hairlike structures that line the nose.

diaphragm a muscular sheet that separates the chest cavity from the abdomen.

exhalation breathing out.

inhalation breathing in.

microbe tiny organism, such as a bacterium or virus, that can cause disease.

organ two or more tissues that work together to do a certain job.

respiration the process by which organisms get and use oxygen.

respiratory system the group of organs that brings oxygen into the body and removes carbon dioxide.

tissue a group of similar cells that do a certain job.

trachea a long tube by which air is carried to and from the lungs.

virus a tiny germ that causes certain infections.

FIND OUT MORE

Books

How Do Your Lungs Work?
 Don L. Curry
 (Children's Press, 2004)

Human Body
 by Richard Walker
 (DK Children, 2009)

Human Body Factory: The Nuts and Bolts of Your Insides
 by Dan Green
 (Kingfisher, 2012)

Lungs: Your Respiratory System
 by Seymour Simon
 (HarperCollins, 2007)

Start Exploring: Gray's Anatomy: A Fact-Filled Coloring Book
 by Freddy Stark
 (Running Press Kids, 2011)

The Lungs and Breathing
 by Carol Ballard
 (KidHaven, 2005)

The Remarkable Respiratory System: How Do My Lungs Work?
 by John Burstein
 (Crabtree, 2009)

The Respiratory System
 by Christine Taylor-Butler
 (Children's Press, 2008)

The Way We Work
 by David Macaulay
 (Houghton Mifflin/Walter Lorraine Books, 2008)

Websites

Allergy Learning Games For Kids
 http://www.learninggamesforkids.com/
 health_games_allergies.html
 Learn about allergies with a word definition matching quiz and other fun games that blend life science with other skills.

Biology 4 Kids: Respiratory System
 http://www.biology4kids.com/files/
 systems_respiratory.html
 Get an in-depth education on all of the parts that make up the respiratory system.

E-Learning for Kids: The Respiratory System
 http://www.e-learningforkids.org/Courses/
 Liquid_Animation/Body_Parts/Respiratory
 _System/
 Take a peek inside your respiratory system in this clickable lesson with bonus comprehension exercises.

Kids Biology: Respiratory System
 http://www.kidsbiology.com/human_biology/
 respiratory-system.php
 Learn all about the respiratory system by watching a short video and reading fact-filled articles complete with images of the body's organs.

Kids Health: How the Body Works
 http://kidshealth.org/kid/htbw/
 Select a body part to watch a video, play a word find, or read an article to learn more about its function in the human body.

NeoK12: Respiratory System
 http://www.neok12.com/Respiratory-System
 .htm
 Watch videos that illustrate the flow of the respiratory system, and then take grade-specific quizzes to test your knowledge.

Science Kids: Human Body for Kids
 http://www.sciencekids.co.nz/humanbody.html
 Sample a range of educational games, challenging experiments, and mind-bending quizzes all while learning about human body topics.

INDEX

allergy, 26
altitude, 16-19
alveoli, 13-15
antibiotics, 25
asthma, 27

bacteria, 11, 20, 25
blood, 14-15
blood vessels, 14
bones, 7-9
breathing. See respiration
bronchi, 6, 12, 27
bronchioles, 12-13

capillaries, 14
carbon dioxide, 5, 15
cells, 5, 11, 24
chest cavity, 7, 8
cilia, 11, 22
circulatory system, 15
coughing, 21-23

diaphragm, 7-9, 21
disease, 11, 20-27

exercise, 16-19, 28
exhalation, 8-9, 15

flu, 24

germs. See microbes

heart, 14, 19

inhalation, 8, 13

lungs, 4-5
    altitude and, 19
    defenses of, 20-23

inhaling and exhaling, 8-9
in respiratory system, 6, 15
problems with, 24-27
structure of, 12-13

microbes, 11, 20-23
Mount Everest, 18
mouth, 6, 15, 20-22
mucus, 10, 11, 20, 22-23
muscles, 7-9, 16

nose, 6, 10-11, 15, 20-22

organs, 6
oxygen, 4-5, 14-19

pneumonia, 25
pollen, 26

respiration, 4-5
    actions in, 8-9
    altitude and, 16-19
respiratory system, 5
    keeping healthy, 28-29
    parts of, 6-7
ribs, 7-9

sneezing, 21-23, 26
stomach, 21, 23

tissues, 8-9, 16
trachea, 6, 12, 22

viruses, 20-21, 24

windpipe. See trachea

CPSIA information can be obtained
at www.ICGtesting.com
Printed in the USA
LVHW072325301018
595431LV00019B/87/P